Also by Bob Hartman:
The Busy Builders
Bob Hartman's Rhyming Bible
The Link-it-Up Bible
The Tell-it-Together Gospel

The Lion Storyteller Bible 25th Anniversary Edition
Welcome to the Journey
Where Do I Come from?

Forthcoming:
Bob Hartman's Rhyming Christmas
The Fantastic Feast
One Sheep Short

———

The original version of this story is found in the Gospel of Matthew, where Jesus says:
'The Kingdom of Heaven is like a merchant on the lookout for choice pearls. When he discovered a
pearl of great value, he sold everything he owned and bought it!'
Matthew 13.45–46 (New Living Translation)

———

First published in Great Britain in 2021

Society for Promoting Christian Knowledge
36 Causton Street, London SW1P 4ST
www.spck.org.uk

British Library Cataloguing-in-Publication Data
A catalogue record for this book is avaliable from the British Library

ISBN 978–0–281–08508–8

Printed by Imago

Produced on paper from sustainable forests

Bob Hartman

THE PRECIOUS PEARL

Fantastic illustrations by

Mark Beech

spck

A merchant found a shiny **PEARL**
the best **PEARL** in the whole **W I D E** world!

So off he went, and off he dashed,
to sell his things and raise some cash.

Did he sell his jars and jugs?

Did he sell his plates and mugs?

Yes, he sold his jars and jugs.

Yes, he sold his plates and mugs

to raise the cash to buy that **PEARL**

the best **PEARL** in the whole **W I D E** world!

And did he sell his billy goat?

Did he sell his fishing boat?

Yes, he sold his
billy goat.

Yes, he sold his
fishing boat.

Yes, he sold his
jars and jugs.

Yes, he sold his plates and mugs

to raise the cash to buy that **PEARL**

the best **PEARL** in the whole **W I D E** world!

And did he sell
his crop of figs?

14

Did he sell his wife's best wigs?

15

Yes, he sold his crop of figs.

Yes, he sold his wife's best wigs.

Yes, he sold his billy goat.

Yes, he sold his fishing boat.

Yes, he sold his jars and jugs.   Yes, he sold his plates and mugs

to raise the cash to buy that **PEARL**   the best **PEARL** in the whole **W I D E** world!

And did he sell his fancy clothes

every stitch of every robe?

Yes, he sold his fancy clothes,
every stitch of every robe.
Yes, he sold his crop of figs.
Yes, he sold his wife's best wigs.
Yes, he sold his billy goat.
Yes, he sold his fishing boat.
Yes, he sold his jars and jugs.
Yes, he sold his plates and mugs

to raise the cash to buy that **PEARL**

the best **PEARL** in the whole **W I D E** world!

And did he sell his farm and land?

His cow called Pat, his sheep called Dan?

Yes he sold his farm and land

his cow called Pat, his sheep called Dan

Yes, he sold his fancy clothes, every stitch of every robe.

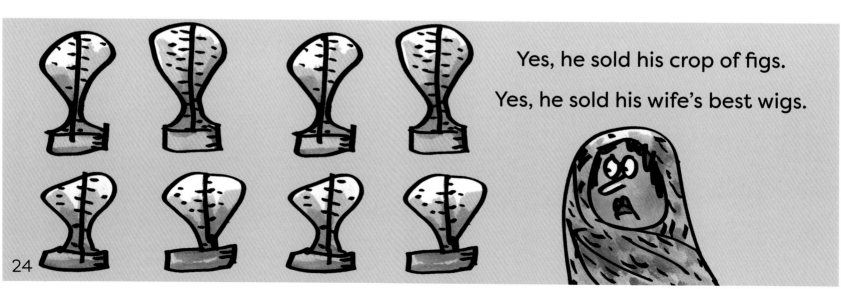

Yes, he sold his crop of figs.

Yes, he sold his wife's best wigs.

Yes, he sold his billy goat.

Yes, he sold his fishing boat.

Yes, he sold his jars and jugs.

Yes, he sold his plates and mugs

to raise the cash to buy that **PEARL**

the best **PEARL** in the whole **W I D E** world!

And did he sell his house and home

and every other
thing he owned?

27

Yes, he sold his house and home
and every other thing he owned.
Yes he sold his farm and land
his cow called Pat, his sheep called Dan.

Yes, he sold his fancy clothes,
every stitch of every robe.
Yes, he sold his crop of figs.
Yes, he sold his wife's best wigs.

Yes, he sold his billy goat.
Yes, he sold his fishing boat.
Yes, he sold his jars and jugs.
Yes, he sold his plates and mugs

to raise the cash to buy that **PEARL**

the best **PEARL** in the whole **W I D E** world!

For God's own kingdom is that **PEARL**

The best thing in the **WHOLE W I D E WORLD**

30

worth letting go of all we hold,

said Jesus in a tale he told.